# Neural Networks

## Step-by-Step

————— ✥❧✥❧ —————

*Understand How Neural Networks Work,*
*Starting With Simple Ideas*

**Matthew Harper**

Additionally, the information in the following pages is intended only for informational purposes and should thus be thought of as universal. As befitting its nature, it is presented without assurance regarding its prolonged validity or interim quality. Trademarks are mentioned without written consent and can in no way be considered an endorsement from the trademark holder.

# Table of Contents

# Introduction

Congratulations on downloading *Neural Networks Step-by-Step: Understand How Neural Networks work, Starting with Simple Ideas* and thank you for doing so.

The concept of artificial intelligence is definitely not a new one. The idea of a machine that can think for itself, make decisions, and plan its own course of actions have been burned into our consciousness from the time we were small children. No matter what your age or where you come from these thoughts inserted themselves into our minds decades ago.

It was first introduced to us through exciting TV shows as science fiction. The "What if" idea of a world where human beings are not the only ones with the capacity to observe their environment, analyze situations, make predictions, and decide on a course of action was initially a mere figment of someone's imagination. But isn't imagination the basis for every great idea that the world has ever embraced? Absolutely, and while it may have seemed unbelievable fifty or sixty years ago, the ability for a machine to do all of these things is not so far out of reach now. In fact, in many cases, the future is already here.

Throughout our history, mankind has created an array of amazing inventions that the world first witnessed through fearful eyes, which they later scrutinized with burning questions then caution, before finally embracing them.

Telephones were once thought of as conduits of evil spirits, yet today people can't leave home without them. Televisions were once thought to emit dangerous X-rays that could harm your health and make you go blind, yet nearly every household has at least one and most have several. When computers were first introduced, they were met with ridicule. Thomas Watson, the Chairman and CEO of IBM commented that "There is a world market for about five computers."

All of these inventions and countless more were not readily accepted by the masses. For many, it took decades for their true capabilities to be appreciated. Were people lacking in vision or did they not appreciate the potential that these wonderful devices had to offer? No. In time, they all came to realize the immense value these devices had. The problem was not lacking in vision nor was it their lack of understanding of what these things could do. Many who ridiculed these things saw first-hand how they worked.

The problem these new ideas faced was trying to get people to understand a device that was before its time. People could only see what was right in front of them and to promote a device, that's clearly meant for the future, in front of people who had never seen it before is rather difficult. No wonder the world ridiculed the idea of a machine thinking for itself because it seemed to be the stuff of fairy tales.

But a machine capable of learning is already here, it is real and it is exciting. Many may not be aware of it but it is already an important role in our lives in many ways. Ever wonder how all those lists of websites can come up so quickly when you do a Google search? What about how Amazon knows exactly what to recommend to you every time you visit their website? And what about how Netflix can choose a list of shows that suit your taste perfectly?

You didn't really think there were a bunch of people picking up your search request and creating these things on their own did you? The fact is that all of these things were done by artificial intelligence, machines programmed to do the grunt work for the masses. Basically, these are computers designed to perform certain functions that make our lives faster, efficient, and more convenient.

How these computers are capable of doing all of these things is the subject of this book. Using this book as a guide, we'll come to understand how the art of neural networks has made it possible for computer science to turn in a whole new direction, opening the doors to an amazing new era of technology. Even as a novice in this industry, you will understand the basics of what neural networks are, how they work, and the many tasks you can apply them to.

We live in exciting times, and the world as we know it is changing quickly. Machine learning is already a hot topic with amazing promises for everyone. It doesn't matter if you're planning to create your own neural network or if you're just attempting to get a better understanding of it. Our goal here is to give you all the information you need to understand how this technology is evolving and give you some guidelines to help you find your place in it. This way, you can decide for yourself whether you want to create your own neural network or if you just want to stand on the sidelines and reap the benefits of this amazing, ground-breaking technology.

There are plenty of books on this subject on the market, so thanks again for choosing this one! Every effort was made to ensure it is full of as much useful information as possible, please enjoy!

# Chapter 1:
# First, Machine Learning

D o you remember when you got your first computer? For most people, the device was so foreign to them they couldn't even understand what they were supposed to do with it. No doubt, for many people, they still wanted one even if they had no idea what its true purpose was. Even today, there are numerous people who have found computers nothing more than a great device for playing games, binge-watching their favorite TV shows, or streaming their favorite music.

But you can do so many amazing things if you know how to tap into the true potential of these wonderful devices. Once a person knows what to do with modern day machines, things begin to change in very big ways. We can easily take a task and go beyond the basics. When that happens, computers become far more than a glorified calculator that can decipher calculations and numbers in a fraction of a second. To get to that point there are a few things that you must understand.

Machines now do not have to have every detail of their functions automatically programmed. They can be programmed to learn a number of tasks and make the necessary adjustments to perform the functions that will allow them to work more efficiently.

Frankly, there are certain computer functions that many assume to be advanced technology but are merely things that can be done very quickly. For example, at the heart of every computer is a very complex calculator. When the computer performs an action we think is fascinating, it is merely the machine performing a number of mathematical equations to produce the results we desire.

You might want to stream your favorite movie to your computer. You click a few buttons and in a matter of seconds, scenes begin to play out in front of your eyes. Really, this function is nothing more than the computer running a bunch of basic math problems in the background, taking the sums and reconstructing them into a video on your screen.

The formulas used are pretty basic, most of them are not different from what you learned in high school. The difference is that computers can do them much faster than we can with our human minds. Even if we are the best at figuring out these types of math problems, humans can never calculate them as quickly as a computer can. Our minds aren't built that way. While it may take us a minute or so to calculate a few numbers in our head, computers have the capability of figuring out millions of equations in a fraction of the time.

But that does not mean that computers are an improved version of the human mind. There are things that the human mind can do equally fast that computers have yet to figure out. Actions like pattern recognition, unstructured problem solving and functioning in 3-dimensional space. Yes, more advanced computers can perform these types of tasks and solve problems, but they have to be given structure and parameters in areas where rules must be followed. Human minds are flexible enough to adapt their thinking to varying circumstances in a vast array of areas. Yes, computers can operate cars and come to quick conclusions, but they have difficulty multitasking and maneuvering in areas without bumping into things or encountering an error.

However, with each passing year, the latest computers are capable of doing more and more things that they could never do in the past. It seems to be just a matter of time before they will one day be capable of doing everything that humans can do but much faster and far more efficiently.

This may seem like science fiction but the possibility is all too real, thanks to the creation of neural networks. In its simplest of terms, neural networks are a series of mathematical formulas called algorithms that identify relationships in a group of data. The network can accomplish this by mimicking the human brain and how it works.

These are complicated networks that are capable of adapting to constantly changing data so that it can achieve the best results possible without having to redesign the criteria needed to get the optimum output.

To put it more simply, neural networks are the means of injecting flexibility into a computer system so that it processes data in a way that is similar to how the human brain works. Of course, computers are still going to be made in the same way as other machines but with each improvement, they are getting closer and closer to thinking machines rather than devices that are strictly following a static set of instructions.

Before we can fully understand neural networks, we have to get a firm grasp on what we mean when we talk about a machine that can learn. We are not talking about giving machines textbooks, homework, and exams so they can learn in the same way a student does. That would be ridiculous, but it helps to see just how a computer can mimic the human brain. So, let's look at how the human brain works first and make a comparison.

When a human being absorbs new information, they usually gain the information from something they're not familiar with. It could come in the form of a question or a statement of something new, or it could come as an experience with no verbal connection whatsoever. The information is picked up through the body's five senses and transmitted directly to the brain. The brain then reshuffles a number of its neural pathways (we call this thinking) so it can process the information and then when all the details related to the information is compared and analyzed in the brain, an answer or a conclusion is drawn and instructions are sent out to the rest of the body.

Since computers don't really think, they have to accomplish the same goal but in a different way. Information is inputted into the computer's programming, it is then processed, calculated, and analyzed based on a number of preset algorithms, and then a conclusion, prediction, or answer is drawn and it comes out as output.

Let's look at an example. Let's say you want to figure out the answer to the problem 7 - 6. This is a basic math question that will require you to 'think' in order to get the right answer. While we will do this very quickly, we need to understand what is happening in our brain so we can see the similarity with computers.

When we receive information, our senses automatically send all the data relating to it to the brain. The brain is made up of billions of neurons that are all interconnected, creating miles upon miles of pathways where information can travel. What's really neat about our brain is that these pathways are constantly shifting based on the data that is being transmitted. When new information is received, they will shift to create new pathways to transmit it to where it needs to go in the brain. Throughout this process, this shifting will continue until a solution is decided upon. Then instructions are sent throughout the body's central nervous system to different parts of the body instructing them on the proper way to respond to the information received. The brain accomplishes all of this in fractions of a second.

In a neural network, the same thing happens. While these networks cannot perfectly mimic the inner workings of the brain, the process is very similar. The information is taken in and the neural network does all the work of consuming data, processing it, and coming up with a workable solution. These networks allow the computer to 'learn' by using algorithms.

## What are algorithms?

No doubt, you've heard the term before. It is often associated with all sorts of technical mechanics but in recent years algorithms are being used in the development of automatic learning, the field that is leading us to advancements in artificial and computational intelligence. This is a method of analyzing data in a way that makes it possible for machines to analyze and process data. With this type of data, computers can work out and perform a number of tasks it could not originally do. They can understand different concepts, make choices, and predict possibilities for the future.

To do this, the algorithms have to be flexible enough to adapt and make adjustments when new data is presented. They are therefore able to give the needed solution without having to create a specific code to solve a problem. Instead of programming a rigid code into the system, the relevant data becomes part of the algorithm which in turn, allows the machine to create its own reasoning based on the data provided.

## How does this work?

This might sound a little confusing but we'll try to break this down into certain examples you can relate to. One of the 'learning' functions of machines is the ability to classify information. To do this, the input data can be a mix of all types of information. The algorithm needs to identify the different elements of the data and then group them into several different categories based on characteristics of similarities, differences, and other factors.

These characteristics can be any number of things ranging from identifying handwriting samples to the types of documents received. If this were code, the machine could only do one single function but because it is an algorithm which can be altered to fit a wide variety of things, the computer can receive this data and classify all sorts of groups that fit within the specific parameters of the circumstances.

This is how machines can change their functions to adapt to the situation at hand. Your email account can analyze all the emails you received, based on a pattern that you have followed, and it divides them into different groups. It can identify which emails are important and you should see right away, those that are spam and junk mail, and even sort out those that may pose a risk to your computer because it carries a virus or malware.

With these types of algorithms, machines can now learn by observing your habits and patterns and adjust their behavior accordingly. So, the very secret to a successful and effective neural pathway depends a great deal on the algorithms your system uses.

# Types of algorithms

Without algorithms, machines cannot learn. So, over the years many different ones have been developed. Depending on what you want your machine to do, they can be grouped into two different categories: supervised and unsupervised.

## Supervised

A supervised algorithm requires a detailed input of related data over a period of time. Once all the information is available to the computer, it is used to classify any new data relating to it. The computer then does a series of calculations, comparisons, and analysis before it makes a decision.

This type of algorithm requires an extensive amount of information to be programmed into the system so that the computer can make the right decision. That way, when it needs to solve a problem, it will attempt to determine which mathematical function it needs to use in order to find the correct solution. With the right series of algorithms already programmed into the system, the machine can sift through all types of data in order to find the solution to a wide variety of problems in the related category.

Supervised algorithms are referred that way because they require human input to ensure that the computer has the right data to process the information it receives.

## Unsupervised

An unsupervised algorithm implies that the computer does not have all the information to make a decision. Maybe it has some of the data needed but one or two factors may be missing. This is kind of like the algebra problems you encountered in school. You may have two factors in the problem but you must solve the third on your own. $A + b = c$. If you know $A$ but you have no idea what $b$ is then you need to plug the information into an equation to solve the problem.

With unsupervised learning, this can be an extremely complex type of problem to solve. For this type of problem, you'll need an algorithm that recognizes various elements of a problem and can incorporate that into the equation. Another type of algorithm will look for any inconsistencies in the data and try to solve the problem by analyzing those.

Unsupervised algorithms clearly are much more complex than the supervised algorithms. While they may start with some data to solve a problem, they do not have all the information so they must be equipped with the tools to find those missing elements without having a human to provide all the pieces of the puzzle for them.

Aside from the two major types of algorithms, there are a number of other types that might be used to teach a machine to learn.

## Reinforcement learning

This type of algorithm allows the system to interact with the environment in an effort to attain a certain goal. Reinforcement learning is commonly used in video games where the computer must navigate and adjust its movements in order to win the game. A reward system is used so the computer knows and understands when it should make the right move, but there are also negative consequences whenever they make errors. This type of algorithm works best in situations where the computer has an obstacle that it must overcome like a rival in a game, or it could also be a self-driving car that needs to reach its destination. The entire focus of the computer is to accomplish certain tasks while navigating the unpredictable environment around it. With each mistake, the computer will readjust its moves in order to reduce the number of errors so it can achieve the desired result.

## Semi-supervised learning

Semi-supervised learning is a blend of both supervised and reinforcement learning. The computer is given an incomplete set of data from which to work. Some of the data include specific examples of previous decisions made with the available data while other data is missing completely. These algorithms work on solving a specific problem or performing very specific functions that will help them achieve their goals.

Of course, these are not the only algorithms that can be used in a computer program to help the machine learning. But, the general idea is the same. The algorithm must fit with the problem the computer needs to solve.

With artificial neural networks applying these different 'secret formulas' many computers can perform functions, solve problems, and carry on a vast variety of learning processes they could not be capable of doing. This field of computer programming is termed 'deep learning,' a subset of machine learning that makes up the foundation of the material contained in this book.

# Chapter 2:
# What Is a Neural Network?

We have already pointed out that these algorithms are an integral part of machine learning. They are used to sift through all sorts of data, pull 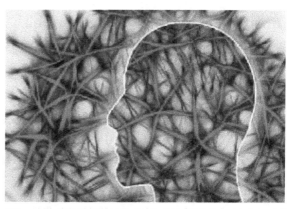 out any information that could be useful to reach the targeted goal and bring you to the closest possible solution to a problem. All of this is done without having to write a specific code for the computer to actually solve the problem because of something called a 'neural network.'

But what exactly is a neural network? Let's go back and take another look at the human brain so we can get a better understanding of this new technology.

The brain holds billions of tiny little neurons that are poised to receive data and process it. These neurons are all interconnected through a complex web with each neuron holding a certain amount of information. These neurons send signals to each other as they process the data they receive.

In a computer, a neural network is created artificially. The architecture has been around for decades but the technology has advanced enough just recently for it to be implemented into any usable and functional form.

In an artificial neural network (ANN) these neurons are mimicked by thousands (sometimes millions) of tiny little processing units, all linked together. Each one of these artificial neurons has a purpose, which is determined by the configuration or the topology of the network.

There are several layers of these neurons and each layer has its own specific purpose. There is the input layer, where all the data flows into the network, the output layer where the solution is produced, and there could be numerous hidden layers where much of the processing work is done.

## The concepts behind neural networks

Back when these networks were originally created, the structures were much simpler than they are today. They consisted of only a few internal units while in today's technological age, each network could literally have millions of tiny little units each perfectly capable of understanding and mastering extremely complex patterns to function properly. The combined efforts of all of these nodes make it possible for the computer to analyze the data it receives, process it, find any type of inconsistencies, and produce a satisfactory result.

We already understand that computers use processors and memory to perform complex computations very quickly. The problem with this system is that they are not capable of adapting to varying forms of input. By utilizing neural networks, computers now have an alternative means of addressing problems.

Their underlying concept can be easily understood when it is compared to the way the physical brain works. In a physical human brain, there is an internal computer that holds approximately $10^{11}$ tiny little transistors. These are small little switches that can turn on or off on command. They respond very quickly to input data with a switching time of around $10^3$ seconds, which is incredibly fast.

Our brains receive and process information in three stages. The senses are feeding the brain with information on a continuous basis. It never stops as shown in the diagram below.

Sense organs receive information through taste, sight, touch, smell, and sound

Information is then sent to the central nervous system, which consists of the brain and/or the spinal cord

Information is processed and instructions are sent to other parts of the body to produce an appropriate response

As you can see, information is continually flowing in one direction. But the function of a physical neural network is much more complicated. A neural network is an attempt to recreate this process in computers. The diagram above, of course, is a highly simplified view of how the brain works. In reality, it is highly complex in how it operates and consists of many parts that all work in harmony in order to accurately simulate thought and learning.

A neural network does not even come close to duplicating the learning process of the brain but its function is based on the basic fundamentals of how the brain operates.

In a typical biological neural network, the key components are the neurons. In a computer system, these are referred to as units (or nodes). Each of these nodes can:

- Receive input from other neurons within its network

- Adapt its internal state to the data received

- Duplicate or create a response signal to send to other neurons within the network

When a neuron receives data, it is transmitted through a series of electrical impulses. The data is encoded based on the period and the recurrence of each of these impulses. In a biological neural network, one neuron can be directly connected to as many as 10,000 other neurons, with each neuron establishing its own pathways and the flow of information based on the impulses received. An artificial neural network attempts to achieve the same results by making the same type of adaptive changes through simulation. To help understand this process, let's have a look at the different components of a neural network in action:

- **Input**

  Input is data received from the external environment. This could be a pattern, a word, or an image. This data is entered into the system and is mathematically designated by the notation $X_i$ *for* $I$ in {*1, n*} where *n* equals the number of inputs.

- **Weights**

  Weights show the strength of the connections between the neurons within the neural network. Every piece of data input must be multiplied by the weights, designated by the symbol $w_i$. After the inputs are all weighed, they are then summed up within the artificial neuron.

- **Sum**

  The sum is given a numerical value, which can range anywhere from zero to infinity. However, the computer will have to limit the response to a set of parameters in order to arrive at a workable value. To accomplish this, a threshold value is established and the sum must be put through an activation function, which is responsible for adjustments based on the data, allowing it to be transformed into the desired output.

## Activation functions

The final stage of processing in an artificial neural network is the activation function where it will take the weighted sum of the input data, add bias, then determine whether or not the data is applicable to the problem and should be used or not.

Basically, the **weighted Sum + Bias** determines the importance of the data to the problem the machine is trying to solve. So, how does the machine determine this? By analyzing the value produced by a neuron to decide if any outside connections should view the neuron as 'fired' or not. Let's try to see this in action:

$Y = \sum (weight * input) + bias$

Here, the value of $Y$ can be any value from *-infinity to +infinity*. At this point, the neuron does not know the limits of the value which means it won't be able to decide if the neuron should be fired or not. In the biological brain, electronic impulses will fire when a neuron should be stimulated because of the data it receives. In other words, it activates.

In a computer, this same process is done through several steps:

- A threshold is established. If the value of Y is above this threshold, it is declared activated. If it falls below this threshold, it will not.

*If Y > threshold = A (activated)*

This type of formula is referred to as a 'step function.' If the output is 1, the neuron is activated when the value is > *0* (threshold) and if the output is 0 it is not activated.

This works well in many cases but not always. This function works best when dealing with strictly 'yes or no' questions. However, in more advanced machines, there may be a need to introduce multiple neurons to connect in order to bring in more classifications of data. In that case, this system would be too basic. It may activate too many neurons, making it very difficult to come up with the best solution to the task.

Ideally, the computer should only activate one neuron to properly solve the problem. In this case, you would need a function that works at activating several different neurons and then choosing those neurons that showed the highest activation rate in comparison to the others.

In a case such as this, a linear function is better suited.

$A = cx$

This type of activation function is based on a straight line where activation is measured in proportion to the input. With this formula, if several neurons activate, the computer can get a range where they can connect them together and then choose the one that has the maximum activation.

But even this formula won't work in every case. There will be situations where there are connected layers and if each layer is activated using this formula, the activation will be passed on to the next level using the result of this formula as an input. That means that no matter how many layers there are they could be replaced by a single layer. In essence, the benefit of the layers and their computations will be invalid. The result will always be the same as with a single layer.

To avoid this problem, there is the sigmoid activation function.

$A - 1/1+e^{-x}$

This type of activation function is nonlinear in nature. The combinations it uses are also nonlinear. It works better when stacking layers. It is also non-binary, so it will provide an analog activation that is different from a step function.

When $X$ values range from -2 to 2, the $Y$ values can be very steep. This means that any small changes in the value of $X$ in that region of the network will automatically cause the values of $Y$ to change as well. This means that the function is very likely to bring the $Y$ values to either edge of the curve, making it a good classifier. This formula is great for creating clear distinctions on predictions.

This is probably why the sigmoid function is one of the most widely accepted functions in use today. But even it has problems.

As you can see, there have to be quite a few different activation functions used in order to ensure that the output of a neural network yields the results needed. Because of the constant variation of data received, there are many different formulas that will allow the computer to learn from its environment.

Since all these activation functions work with different types of data, it can be difficult to know which formula to use. If the system knows the characteristics of the data, it can easily choose the activation function that will yield the results faster. But as the data makes its way through the network, several functions have to be applied until the computer gives the most accurate result.

## Architectures

As we begin to understand neural networks better, we begin to formulate an image of a very distinct architecture. Each network has very specific components that are arranged in layers. Most of them have a three-layered architecture but some can have even more.

## Layers

A neural network is divided up into three or more layers, each having a completely different function. These layers are stacked up on top of each other and join up with each other during the artificial learning process.

### Input layers

This is where the data is received. The nodes on the input are passive in the sense that they do not have a function that will allow them to modify data. Their sole purpose is to receive the data from their external environment.

### Output layers

These are responsible for making computations and communicating instructions to the outside environment.

### Hidden layers

A neural network could have one hidden layer or it could have hundreds. Their role is to copy the information the input layer receives and disseminate it to other layers in the network. They also perform calculations and exchange data taken from the input hubs and deliver it to the yield hubs.

Most neural networks are completely interconnected so that every neuron is connected to every other neuron on the previous layer before it and to the layer above it. This way, the input layer is always connected to the hidden layer, and the hidden layer is always connected to the output layer.

This layering is also found in the human brain. However, the human brain literally contains billions of neurons fully interconnected whereas a computer system may only have thousands or millions at the most. It is this unique architecture that makes it possible for computers to mimic the thinking process and actually learn new information without having to have all the data entered into their programs.

# Chapter 3:
# Technical Fields and How They Operate

Even the most advanced neural networks are pretty primitive when compared to the human brain. They tend to process information one at a time whereas the biological brain can easily multitask, capable of doing several things at once and that's all without having to burn extra energy to get it done.

Think of what you do every day. You can prepare a meal, have a conversation, and fill out your shopping list all at the same time. If you work in an office, you may be typing a letter, taking phone calls, and doing research altogether. In comparison, the artificial neural networks generally 'learn' by comparing one classification of a record with another classification. When there are errors that result from this process, they will readjust their formula and modify the algorithm and repeat the process, each time reducing the rate of error until they find a solution that best matches the task at hand.

## Training the neural network

Let's look at this process in a bit more detail. First by looking at what a neural network is really comprised of.

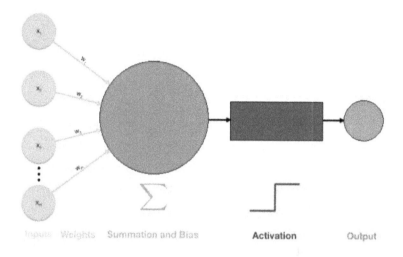

Inputs  Weights  Summation and Bias          Activation        Output

1. A set of input values and their weights.

2. A function that calculates the sum of the weights and then maps the results to an output

These two elements and how they work together can be seen clearly in the diagram below.

As you can see, the neurons on the input level receive the data input. The hidden layer directly above the input layer copies the data and any weights associated with it. Then these sums are totaled up and measured against known biases before the data is passed on to an activation layer where the decision will be made to fire the neuron or not. If the neuron is fired, then an appropriate output is determined, which will send a signal to the external environment dictating what action, if any, should be taken.

To visualize this better, it helps to know that there are no physical neurons on the different layers but rather a compilation of coded values contained in a data record. The next layer or series of layers are the hidden layers, where most of the computations will be performed, and the final layer or the output layer contains a single node for each class. As the data passes through the network, every node in the output layer is assigned a specific value, and the record is awarded to the node that contains the highest value.

In supervised training, during the training phase, each record has a known value so the output nodes can be assigned the correct values. A "1" is assigned to the node with the correct class and a "0" for all the others. This way, the computer can compare the calculated values with the correct values and determine the percentage of error for each node. This is called the Delta Rule.

## The delta rule

Sometimes referred to as the 'least mean square method,' the delta rule is probably the most commonly used rule in training a neural network. With every input vector, the system compares the output vector to the correct solution. If the difference is 0, it means that the system learned nothing in the process. If the value is anything other than zero, the system automatically goes back to the weights associated with the input data and makes adjustments to bring the difference closer to zero.

For example, if you wanted to calculate the answer for 3 x 4, the computer will likely process the information as 4 + 4 + 4 and give you an output of 12. This is pretty basic thinking and both human brains and neural networks can get the result in a matter of seconds. However, let's suppose the problem is a bit more complex.

Perhaps we don't know the right formula to calculate the right answer. All we know is that the information is linear, which means that if one number in the equation is doubled, the other number must also be doubled. In a biological brain, this type of linear thinking is called 'intuition.'

The relationship between the different factors gives an indication of what needs to be done. The computer will apply an equation which reflects that relationship to solve the problem.

The only other data the system will have could be some examples that multiply numbers together to get the correct value. This data stored in the memory banks give real evidence that shows exactly how to arrive at the correct answer. The program will then process that calculation and compare it to the data it already has. If the difference is off, it will go back and make adjustments and then recalculate to solve for a better answer. It will continue to do this until it gets an answer that is either exact or close enough that it cannot reduce the error rate any longer.

The network 'learns' by checking the error rate and continuously readjusting until it gets to the right solution. This continuous refinement of the answer as a means to get to the nearest point of the correct answer is the simplest form of training the neural network.

There are many algorithms that are already programmed into the system that can be called upon to find the right solution to a given problem. These algorithms are chosen based on the type of problem the computer needs to solve.

## Clustering

But how can we get a network to classify data rather than calculate it? This simply requires using a different type of algorithm. Let's say you have images of dogs and birds all mixed together and you want the computer to separate those images. In a biological brain, you can tell in a fraction of a second which ones are cats and which ones are dogs, but this is something a computer can't do.

This almost the same general process of repeating the algorithm and constantly refining the answer until you have successfully completed the task. However, in the case of classification, the network doesn't need to come up with some type of mathematical theory to solve the problem. Instead, it relies on some examples to guide its choices.

The data received may detail specific characteristics of dogs and birds. These are characteristics that are common knowledge and everyone knows to be true. These details are referred to as the 'training data.' Of course, the data needs to be in a language that the computer can understand. Descriptions such as "A dog has four legs, a tail, and pointed ears" will not do. Instead, the input data will be in the form of a table or a graph.

| Example | Width | Length | Features | Classification |
|---------|-------|--------|----------|----------------|
| 1 | 6" - 24' | 1' - 5' | Hair | Dog |
| 2 | 2" - 2' | 5" - 3' | Feathers | Bird |

The network will use this set of examples to plot a slope separating any data that matches the criteria. It will begin with a random division so that it has a baseline to work with. It will then check its answers against the known truths it already has to see how close it is to the correct division. Then it will repeat the process over and over again until it reaches the right solution. This process is called 'clustering' and is used for classifying different things, and for making predictions based on data received.

Once the correct result is attained, the data is stored in the memory banks and is used as an example the next time another problem like this comes up. In this way, the computer actually 'learns.'

These are not the only ways a neural network can learn but as you can see from the examples, the process is very basic. It is important, however, to understand that when the system has to figure out a problem with multiple elements in it, each hidden layer in the network can only perform one function. So, an extremely complex problem may require many hidden layers in order to come up with the right solution.

To put it simply, these programs cannot read words so basic mathematical algorithms are used to determine the relationship between the output error of a problem and the correct answer (or a solution that will solve the problem). This process is repeated over and over again, refining the answer until it reaches a point where it cannot be improved any further. In order for this to be accomplished, the neural network must be set up with real-world examples of data that is known to be true and accurate. If the data the system relies on is not accurate it is not possible for the computer to learn and expand that knowledge.

# Chapter 4:
# What Is It Used for and How?

There is a great deal of excitement surrounding this new technology. With each new advancement, machine learning is gradually moving closer towards handling the more abstract tasks that up until now, have only been successfully done by humans. It is difficult to convince those who are not familiar with the science of the many tasks that machine learning can accomplish.

The different ways this can be used are endless. In fact, there are probably quite a few applications that are affecting your life right now that you didn't realize were being implemented.

## Deep learning

Even without a background in computer science, one can understand what the term 'machine learning is.' Basically, it is a machine that learns from data. As long as the machine has the right data input there is a huge number of problems that it can solve without any human interference. As long as the machine is given the correct training data and the right algorithms, it can perform the necessary functions and continue to learn from them for an indefinite period of time.

The primary tools at the heart of deep learning are the input data and algorithms. Without the correct data, it is not possible for deep learning to take place. For years, machines have functioned without algorithms but these machines are programmed to perform certain functions without change (think vending machines) which means the program it started out with will not adapt over time. It will still perform the same actions over and over again regardless of the environment that surrounds it.

However, with deep learning, the computer is capable of making continuous adjustments in order to improve its performance every time it is used. But to really grasp the concept of deep learning, we need to take some time and look closely under the hood. Its use today can help us to see how deep learning is already changing our lives for the better.

When we turn on our home PCs we automatically expect things to happen, and we expect them to happen at record speeds without even thinking about what goes into getting the results we want.

When you turn on Netflix, you will quickly see a list of movies, documentaries, and TV shows that you like. You make your choice without thinking about how deep learning machines have studied your choices over the years and came up with options that are more appealing to you. If you like science fiction, miraculously, you will have a host of science fiction options laid out before you. Because the machine has analyzed your entertainment choices you have the best options in front of you to choose from.

Deep learning is also used by Google, to predict what websites you will most likely want to visit. Google's voice and image recognition algorithms are being used in a host of new industries. MIT is now using deep learning to predict events that are most likely to happen in the future. Everywhere you look, deep learning is beginning to permeate all types of industries and expectations are that it will continue to grow in the future.

But for those who don't fully grasp computer science concepts, the thought of deep learning might instill fear instead of excitement. After all, in the past few decades, the subject has been approached with a lot of skepticism and doubt. Movies have portrayed power hungry machines bent on taking over the world, and news reports about every self-functioning machine failure have been exploited to the highest level. It leads some people to believe that machines capable of learning are more of a threat to humanity than a help. So, what exactly is this kind of technology used for and do we really have anything to worry about?

## Classification

Deep learning machines have extremely comprehensive databases and sophisticated networks that allow for easy classification of many different forms of data. We might assume that looking at a picture and identifying its contents is pretty basic stuff. To the human eye, images can be classified in a fraction of a second but to a machine, which only sees things in terms of math, they contain many different elements that must first be sorted out.

Deep learning, however, makes it possible for machines to classify any type of data including video, speech, audio, or handwriting and analyze it to come up with a conclusion that would be similar to that of most humans.

Imagine a computer system that can automatically create a record of the number of vehicles that pass through a certain point on a public road during a set time frame. The steps needed for this to happen are immense. Not only would it have to hold a huge database of different types of cars, their shapes, and sizes but it must also capable of processing the data and analyzing it to come up with an acceptable answer.

Comparing the data it receives through its sensors to the data it has stored in the database, it can classify the answer with a pretty high level of accuracy. While humans could easily identify cars by make and model, the idea of having a human standing on a street corner counting and labeling cars would virtually be impossible to achieve. Even if someone could position themselves to count, humans get tired and need to have frequent breaks. They cannot function continuously without stopping. The level of accuracy would be much lower. Yet, automobile manufacturers, government agencies, and other industries could find the information extremely valuable in making decisions for their business.

But deep learning goes even further than this. While the system may already be programmed with a massive database, as the machine operates it will learn even more and increase its knowledge from its experiences. By being programmed to train itself, continuous human interaction is not necessary. The machine will learn from its mistakes in much the same way as humans do.

**Pattern recognition**

Pattern recognition is probably the oldest form of machine learning but is also the most fundamental. As of 2015, pattern recognition was one of the most popular areas of interest in research labs around the globe. By giving a machine the ability to recognize a character or some other object, the potential for machine learning increased exponentially.

The ability of a machine to recognize handwritten numbers and letters opens the door to a myriad of uses. This ability has been successful in providing insights into the complex movements of the environment, weather changes, and even in the world of finance. But deep learning involves more than just identifying similar characteristics and differences in images. Pattern recognition allows them to draw their own conclusions in regards to the images or videos they are analyzing and tagging them appropriately. Every time they perform this type of analysis, the better it will become at identifying similar situations and unusual anomalies that could affect the outcome.

Right now, the New York City Department of Transportation has joined up with IntelliScape.io to use this technology and get a better understanding of traffic in their area. They can now see patterns in the weather, identify areas where parking violations are more likely to occur, and as a result, inform local officials of these patterns so they can be prepared to respond accordingly.

There are many uses for pattern recognition in many areas. It can be used to expand the 'Internet of Things' by collecting data from any device that is connected to the internet. Cities will use it to understand how people navigate through their streets, urban planners can make better decisions about the location of physical infrastructures and even in the area of conservation, it can be helpful. Instead of using manpower to go out and count trees, drones can be deployed to analyze the number of trees and their health in any given area.

## Prediction

The use of predictions can also be used by many industries. Whether it is in the field of medicine to detect abnormal genes in an unborn child or predicting the change in weather, because of the ability of these machines to paint a realistic picture of future possibilities their potential is huge.

Industries are already using this prediction technology in a vast number of fields.

The pharmaceutical industry uses it to determine the exact set of compounds needed to treat a specific disease. They can now predict which medicines will be more effective and use that data to develop new drugs to fight disease. They can also use it to identify alternative treatments that may also be effective.

In the area of cybersecurity, programs like Deep Instinct focuses on predicting where cyber hackers and other online threats may occur so they can develop ways of protecting the end user before an attack actually happens.

In agriculture, crop outputs can be determined even before planting begins. The computer will analyze weather predictions, soil conditions, and quality of seeds to determine how successful a crop will be and how much profit can be gained.

The same can be said in areas of retail, insurance, finance, and even in aerospace. The potential for this type of technology is vast and positive. As more and more industries begin to adopt deep learning and incorporate it into their business strategies, all sorts of events will become much more efficient and accurate.

Years ago, this type of technology was thought to be in the realm of science fiction and fantasy, but today it is a reality. While computers are a long way from the kind of independent thinking and autonomy that could rule the world, they definitely have come a long way from the vending machine era. The future of neural networks and deep learning are extremely progressive and definitely something we can all look forward to with high anticipation.

# Chapter 5:
# Types of Neural Networks

U p until now, we've discussed the basic principles that support neural networks but you've probably gathered that there is a lot more to it than the basics. There are, in fact, many different types of neural networks, each designed to address a specific type of problem. In this chapter, we'll look at some of these neural networks in order to get a better understanding of their purpose and how they are used.

## Convolutional neural networks

For humans, image recognition is done without thought. It happens almost instantly. We see a photo of our grandmother and we don't have to analyze it to determine who it is, we just know. Every person can identify a bird when they see one. In our brains, this process is second nature but teaching a computer to do it is no easy task.

Computers can do this now with the use of a convolutional neural network. This is a neural network that uses identical replicas of the same neuron. This makes it possible for the network to learn the characteristics of a single neuron and then use it in a variety of different places.

The architecture of a convolutional neural network is based on the biological process that happens when a person identifies something with their sight. In the human eye, individual cortical neurons respond to stimulation from light as it enters the person's field of vision. This is known as the 'receptive field,' which is almost entirely covered by neurons. In a computer, this process is accomplished with convolutional neural networks (CNN).

These are a special class of networks that are enhanced to be extremely powerful in selected fields like image recognition and classification. They can identify objects, signs, and are the primary tool used in modern inventions like self-driving automobiles.

Each CNN has several sub-sampling layers as well as a number of additional layers that are all interconnected. When data input is gathered it is based on a very specific formula that tells the computer the height and the width of the image as well as the number of colors and any other characteristics that will allow the computer to make an identification.

To create a CNN, the computer must be programmed to recognize an object. Any object. Just like with other types of neural networks, computers can solve a number of different problems by linking a series of neurons together. This way, all the neurons work together to calculate the relevant features of the problem. With a CNN, you can use the same algorithms but adapt them to different types of problems. By adapting the algorithm to recognize an object rather than coming up with a numerical calculation you can simplify the task.

CNN's can only work with data, the more data it receives the easier it will accomplish the task. If you want the computer to identify a handwriting sample, it is important to provide it with a large number of handwriting samples to use as a basis for its assumption.

To that end, researchers have already created a dataset of handwritten numbers called the MNIST, which contains more than 60,000 images of handwritten figures. However, computers only recognize numerical values not images, so you will have to transform those images into a matrix of numbers, which symbolizes its different characteristics.

To input this image into a neural network it needs to be transformed from a visual image to a matrix that consists of more than 300 numbers, which should look something like this:

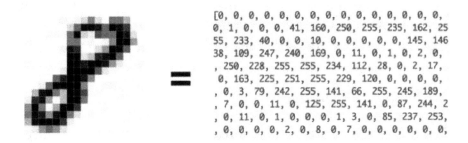

```
[0, 0, 0, 0, 0, 0, 0, 0, 0, 0, 0, 0, 0, 0, 0,
0, 1, 0, 0, 0, 41, 160, 250, 255, 235, 162, 25
55, 233, 40, 0, 0, 10, 0, 0, 0, 0, 0, 145, 146
38, 109, 247, 240, 169, 0, 11, 0, 1, 0, 2, 0,
, 250, 228, 255, 255, 234, 112, 28, 0, 2, 17,
0, 163, 225, 251, 255, 229, 120, 0, 0, 0, 0,
, 0, 3, 79, 242, 255, 141, 66, 255, 245, 189,
, 7, 0, 0, 11, 0, 125, 255, 141, 0, 87, 244, 2
, 0, 11, 0, 1, 0, 0, 0, 1, 3, 0, 85, 237, 253,
, 0, 0, 0, 0, 2, 0, 8, 0, 7, 0, 0, 0, 0, 0, 0,
```

In order to manage all of these inputs, the neural network must be expanded so that it has at least 2 outputs instead of 1. The first output will calculate the probability rate that the picture is a 'number 8' while the other output will do the opposite and calculate the probability that the image is not. The system will then categorize all the images in the database with a separate output for each group of items it will have to identify.

While the neural network is not capable of matching the recognition skills of the human eye, it can recognize objects when properly programmed to do so. This type of function can be very useful in a wide range of industries that need recognition skills in areas where humans cannot function at an extremely rapid pace.

# Perceptron and backpropagation

The most basic and simplest form of a neural network is the perceptron. It has a simple binary function that can produce only two possible results. If the solution it produces is positive the function will produce a 1 but if it is negative the result will be a 0.

This type of network is designed for a very specific class of problems, such as the identification of objects. A single perceptron can identify a dividing line and can tell whether any given point is located above or below that line.

### Multilayer perceptron

Multilayer perceptrons are often used to analyze a large amount of data that exists in table format. They can decipher rows and columns and use them as variables. This system works best when the rows and columns are interchangeable. They can switch them around without risk of changing the meaning or the value of the data.

In an MLP, the input for the classifier is first changed by using a non-linear transformation formula. This places the input data into an area where it can then be separated linearly. This is usually done in one of the hidden layers of the network.

To train an MLP, parameters must be set. These parameters must represent the qualities of the classifications that need to be made. The good news is that in the last few decades, guidelines have been created that make selecting these parameters much simpler. Several of these guidelines already exist and can be found in programs like the Efficient BackProp.

## Backpropagation

Backpropagation was originally introduced back in the 70s but was not fully put to use until later in the 80s. It is a faster method than many other neural networks of its time. It is an algorithm that can be used in supervised learning in many artificial neural networks and can be used to create a gradient descent and as a means of training neural networks.

The method does a calculation to determine the gradient of the error function in relation to the weights. Basically, the concept is that the gradient will move backward through the network so that the last layer of weights is calculated first and those of the first layer are calculated last.

Training with backpropagation uses the gradient descent technique in order to find the updates of the weights. Gradient descent is basically the trial and error method where the rate of error is minimized with each successive iteration (or attempt) in order to lower the percentage of error.

Backpropagation calculates the delta rule when using a multilayer feed-forward network and requires three components:

- A dataset, which comprises input/output pairs

- Feedforward neural networks

- And an error function

The network is trained to give an estimation of the value of a specific function. The system is trained using the dataset to identify a pattern. Afterward, the network will need to give an estimate of the value using the Gaussian function to make an approximation.

To make a time series prediction, the goal is to develop a network that can predict a value on a given time series. This type of network is often used in making stock market predictions or to analyze market trends. In such cases, the input data is given in chunks and the output it yields will become the next piece of data that follows that chunk.

There are, of course, several other types of neural networks that can be applied to a wide number of problem-solving issues. Based on the network's given architecture, the algorithms used, and the quality of the data input, these networks can be applied to a vast number of conditions.

Whether the goal is to identify certain images or to calculate large numbers to come up with a prediction, there is a good chance that the type of neural network needed is already in existence.

# Chapter 6:
# Neural Networks and Artificial Intelligence

Probably the most exciting application of neural networks is its use in artificial intelligence. This sub-niche is the reason why many are waiting in anticipation for the future. While there is no specific definition of this type of technology, almost everyone you meet will have an opinion of what artificial intelligence really means.

Actually, artificial intelligence is a form of science with the primary goal of developing machines that have the ability to continuously increase their intelligence. It is a progressive science that is only made possible because of the creation of neural networks. To do this, scientists must constantly improve on the networks with each new creation. They hope that the machines will get closer and closer to a level of intelligence comparable to humans.

Only humans have the ability to think, analyze, and understand their environment, its actions, and the realities that exist. Only humans can explain their world and think in the abstract. Our brains can take in a wealth of information and draw conclusions in the fraction of a second.

Machines, on the other hand, using the same set of data, will face numerous challenges. For example, today, computers can hold a database of thousands of similar images, assess them and draw a conclusion with 95% efficiency. This is quite impressive by any stretch but still, it cannot explain why it chose the images, ascertain their meaning, or distinguish why one image is different from another. In other words, computers can compute but they can't reason. So, even though they are capable of producing amazing results with the tasks they are given, they still are far behind the ability of the human brain in many ways.

To overcome these obstacles, a unique form of machine learning has been developed. Most of us know it as Artificial Intelligence or AI. The term refers to the simulation of intelligence in machines. Today's machines are programmed to 'think' and mimic the way the human brain operates. These machines are slowly taught to rationalize in given situations, analyze, and choose a course of action that would have the best chance of achieving the optimum goal.

As technology continues to advance, it is only natural that older machines will become outdated. For example, machines that perform basic functions or can recognize and identify text used to be cutting edge but today, they are so obsolete that they are no longer considered to be an artificial intelligence. This is because the function now is taken for granted. This ability has become so commonplace that it is often viewed as a normal computer function.

Computers said to have artificial intelligence today are those that show more impressive abilities like being able to play chess, self-driving cars, and smart homes. Why are these functions given the label of artificial intelligence? For those that can play chess, these machines can win the game against a human opponent, self-driving cars have mastered the ability to absorb all the external data surrounding them and compute it fast enough that they can navigate and reach their destination without causing an accident of some kind. Smart homes can interact with members of the household, control the temperature, manage security, and even food supply to ensure the comfort of its inhabitants.

Of course, when anything completely new is introduced to the world, there is often some skepticism involved and the same could be true in regards to artificial intelligence. Even though we interact with AI on a daily basis, most of us don't realize it. Whenever you talk to SIRI through an Apple device, you're using artificial intelligence. Alexa from Amazon also makes use of the same technology. These devices, though impressive, are considered to be what is called 'narrow AI' or a 'weak AI.' They are only programmed to perform a very small number of tasks. These merely represent the first introductory steps of AI on a long-term goal towards a more human interaction with machines. With that said, aside from the fears that many people have about AI, there are numerous benefits that we will gain from these advantages.

## Artificial intelligence in medicine

When it comes to healthcare, artificial intelligence is already making impressive progress, especially in the field of health. While we have not reached the point of developing a strong AI, artificial intelligence is already a major part of our lives. With a machine capable of thinking and reasoning, treatment of patients will be much more efficient. Physicians will have easy access to all the data they need and these machines will be instrumental in helping them make a good decision.

This type of technology won't be available until sometime far into the future. Currently, many people are creating algorithms that will help them solve many of the problems in healthcare today. We're not looking at 100 or 200 years down the road but more like five to ten years.

Right now, IBM's Watson is leading the pack with its cognitive computing used for healthcare. They are closely followed by neural networks developed by big names such as Dell, Hewlett-Packard, Apple, Hitachi, Digital Reasoning, Sentient Technologies, and more.

With each new advancement made by these companies, health care improves by a greater margin. Right now, there are countless areas in the field of medicine being addressed. We will see progress in the following areas:

- **Data management**

  AI will be primarily responsible for collecting it, storing, it, analyzing it, and drawing conclusions from it. For example, the Google Deepmind Health project is already mining medical records in order to come up with a way to provide better health services for patients. For now, they are working with the Moorfield Eye Hospital NHS Foundation on ways to improve eye treatment.

- IBM's Watson mentioned earlier that its artificial intelligence is working with oncologists to improve the way of analyzing evidence-based treatment options. It has already improved the ability to analyze the meaning and the context of data found in clinical notes and reports. This information, once difficult to decipher, could be very instrumental in finding a workable treatment by combining multiple aspects from a patient's file with external research to identify the best course of treatment. The belief is that one day, Watson may be the best resource for patients struggling with cancer. Watson impressed many by analyzing 3,500 medical textbooks and 400,000 other pieces of related data, all in 17 seconds, to come up with a viable treatment option for the patient. It is expected that Watson will be rolled out to the mainstream population by the end of 2018.

- Another artificial intelligence from IBM is the Medical Sieve. This is an exploratory project that is labeled as a 'cognitive assistant.' This AI analyzes, and reasons on a vast amount of clinical data that is then used in the decision-making process in fields of radiology and cardiology. It can analyze radiology images and identify anomalies that point out health problems much faster than the human eye. In the future, radiologists will only need to view the most complicated of cases where human supervision will be necessary.

- Genetics study will also benefit greatly from artificial intelligence. The Deep Genomics project is at work identifying patterns in a massive compilation of genetic information and medical records. The project is looking for mutations and other anomalies that could help detect diseases very early on. Their work on inventing a whole new generation of computers that will let doctors see what happens inside a cell once the DNA is altered by its genes.

- The Human Genome project is busy developing an algorithm that could make it possible to spot cancer and vascular diseases in the early stages.

- Artificial intelligence will also help in developing pharmaceuticals through clinical trials, which normally take years to develop. By getting through this process many times faster, billions of dollars will be saved and more people will receive treatment for less money.

These are only a few of the examples of artificial intelligence at work today in the healthcare industry. With so much data flooding into the system, it is virtually impossible for humans to sift through it all. Consider the sheer number of patient medical records, treatment data, and all of the other technological devices that are accumulating information about health. All of this could be analyzed in a matter of seconds where it would take humans years to digest it. This means that healthcare will naturally improve and more people will be able to receive faster and better treatment than they have ever had before.

## Artificial intelligence in finance

Another area where artificial intelligence is already making an impression is in the finance industry. As of now, nearly every financial company in the industry is ready to embrace AI. It not only will save them time, it will cut costs, and add value to their services.

A perfect example of this is the AI computer Wealthfront, which tracks user account activity in order to analyze account holder's spending behavior. By understanding this behavior, the company can help them make proper financial decisions and even customize the advice they give to their clients.

As of 2016, more than 550 financial companies have already started using artificial intelligence in their business, generating an additional $5 billion in revenue. In fact, the top seven US commercial banks also are making AI a priority as a means of servicing their customer base better. As a result, they were able to improve performance and generate more income at the same time.

Consider the results generated by JPMorgan Chase's 'Contract Intelligence' platform, which uses AI image recognition software to extract important data from legal documents. Normally, this task would take approximately 360,000 hours of manpower while the AI did it all in a matter of seconds.

Finance is expected to be heavily influenced by artificial intelligence in every aspect. It is already setting the stage for a complete renovation among the industry leaders, making them more competitive in the process. Any company that has not tapped into artificial intelligence will quickly find themselves falling behind in their ability to maximize their resources, lower their risks, increase their revenue streams, increase their ability to trade, invest, lend, and more.

All of this is now being done through automation. Many of the once repetitive tasks are now being handled through neural networks in artificial intelligence. Their software is capable of matching data records, analyzing and looking for exceptions, and placing the decision-making process in the hand of this new technology. Since AI is designed to be a learning machine that will be constantly improving itself, in time they will be able to take over more of the mundane and repetitive jobs that are now consuming many hours of manpower.

Right now, AI in the finance industry is primarily used in three areas:

- Calculating parameters and numbers beyond human capabilities

- Analyzing and interpreting written text by using a special program that allows them to grasp the context of the language used in contracts and agreements

- Pattern recognition to detect different types of activity, audit books, and inspect finances in ways that go beyond human accuracy

The benefits of AI in the finance industry will be better trading by making selections through algorithms, better investment insights, improved risk management, improved fraud detection, and better choices when it comes to making credit decisions.

There are countless applications that are already being put to good use in financial services, and there is more of that to come in the future. So, the next time you need to make an investment decision or receive a recommendation from your financial institution, it's a good bet that you're getting your advice from some form of artificial intelligence.

## Artificial intelligence in translation

Today, there are more than 6,000 languages spoken around the globe. Anytime someone needs to communicate with someone from another language group problems arise. In most cases, if one party does not understand the other, there will be a need for a translator. This is not only time consuming but expensive.

Now though, according to two separate research papers, artificial intelligence is beginning to become a major part of the translation industry. There are now several different AI programs that use unsupervised artificial intelligence that can perform language translation efficiently without the use of a language dictionary. The methods work both with parallel text as well as with identical text that is already being used in other languages.

These programs begin with data specifically chosen to supply them with an extensive bilingual dictionary that they can reference without the aid of a human to verify their answers. The machines rely on the relationship that exists between words. For example, tree and leaves or shoes and socks. These relationships exist in some form in all languages. The AI looks at these words and groups them into clusters and connects them from one language to another to help them understand how the syntax of another language is formed.

The dictionary the computer builds from the data is then put together with two additional AI methods called 'back translation' and 'denoising.' Back translation translates one sentence into the new language and then translates it back again as a way of testing its accuracy. If the back-translated sentence doesn't match the original, the system will automatically readjust its parameters and make a second attempt. It will continue to do this until it gets as close as possible to the correct answer. Denoising works in a similar way but goes an additional step. It randomly removes a word from the sentence to make sure that the AI is also building on the structure of the sentence rather than just translating them word for word.

Google and Facebook both have incorporated language translation into their platform successfully. We can fully expect more artificial intelligence applications in language translation to be introduced in the future.

There is no doubt that machine translation has improved a great deal in recent years. It is much more accurate, it works at impressive speeds, and it is readily available in almost every language you speak.

A good example of this is Google translate. According to their records, the machine translator has an impressive accuracy that is on par with human translators. Every day, it translates Spanish, Chinese, French, as well as many other languages to English and back again both accurately and quickly. As their program continues to learn, it has reached high accuracy levels so it can be relied on in a wide range of business applications. Today, machine translation is being used in government, software and technology, military and defense, healthcare, finance, legal, and E-commerce.

Whether the need is for text to text, text to speech, speech to text, speech to speech, or even an image to text, there is an AI program that can handle it.

# Game playing

While the other applications of artificial intelligence deal with the serious matters of business, money, and health, there is another area where these programs have made a lasting impression that is not always so serious. This is not to say that game playing is not as important as the other industries. In fact, for many, the art of game playing is, in reality, a very serious business.

It would actually be a miscarriage of justice to ignore the gaming industry when talking about modern technology. For many decades now, board games have been at the center of AI research, in more recent years we've witnessed the progression widen out to incorporate video games as well. In fact, video games have become even more sophisticated in many ways mainly because of the introduction of artificial intelligence.

These programs are designed to control non-player characters, generating data about their opponents and adapting to their behaviors. Game developers have realized that using AI programs to analyze large amounts of data generated from players from all over the globe has helped them develop games that are more intricately designed.

While gamers are a small community in comparison with the other major industries, it is growing in popularity mainly because of what they have learned by applying artificial intelligence analysis in their designs.

It is a thriving field of research, but it is also a phenomenal playing field for testing out new algorithms that can one day be adopted into other industries as well. In fact, it is with the gaming industry that AI often introduces new programs that have gone on to increase computational power and generate countless stories of success in many other industries.

Think about some of the common uses for AI today that was actually started and tested first in the gaming world.

- Image and speech recognition

- Emotion detection

- Self-driving cars

- Web searching

- Creative design

All of these concepts that are now part of the real world were first tested in a game of some kind.

All this helps us see just how important the gaming world is to modern technology. Just like many scientific ideas were first introduced to the world through science fiction books, TV shows, and movies, much of the technology that makes them possible was introduced through games.

But what about game playing itself? The fact is, the gaming world is the safest environment where scientific problem solving can work in harmony with creativity. AI helps humans to better understand how we play games, how we understand the interactions between players, and therefore how to build a better game.

But gaming AI is not limited to the board games or even the online versions of many games but is playing a major role in the gaming industry. You know the kind of games that go in Las Vegas, Reno, and Atlantic City? Once upon a time, these were the only locations where one could put money down on a poker game or gamble a little on the turn of a roulette wheel. But because of artificial intelligence, these games can now be played with just as much vigor as you would if you were there in person. Now, poker games are popping up all over the world. You might be sitting across the table with one player in Japan, another in Spain, and another in South Africa.

These types of games have become profitable ventures on all fronts. Many people who would have previously been unknown have become world-renowned players for their winning streaks.

New games have also begun to emerge as a result of artificial intelligence. The game Nevermind, introduced in 2016 is capable of tracking how a player's emotions unfold during the game and adjust its playing strategy accordingly.

Games have been a prominent area for testing AI and will continue to be so. Not only does it provide programmers a safe place to test new algorithms and designs, it is also the one place where there can be true human-computer interactions so we can see how it plays out in the future. The simple fact that games are so popular opens the door to amazing possibilities. People are more willing to test them out, computers have a wealth of data to analyze, and they can create a host of problems and challenges that can be worked out over time.

# Chapter 7:
# Neural Networks in the Future

I t's hard to imagine the possibilities the future holds for neural networks. Because of how this technology is already 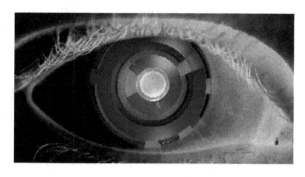 integrating themselves into every aspect of our lives, the potential for new and innovative ideas is higher than ever. We can envision a Jetson-like world where we will have self-driving cars instead of GPS devices that need to be programmed with our intended destination. Imagine a car that has learned your personal preferences in the music you listen to, the temperature you're most comfortable with, and how to perfectly adjust your seat.

But all of that is possible now. The future holds a lot more possibilities where neural networks can be applied.

There are two different ways that this new learning technology can grow. One area is in the field of virtual intelligence. This type of program could be planned, controlled, predictable, and could eventually become the next evolutionary step in artificial intelligence.

This type of intelligence would be even closer to matching its thinking and learning styles to humans. A machine that can evolve and grow with mankind, adapt to the same environment and learn from its experiences is inevitable.

To advance to this point, however, requires technology that can actually understand and make the necessary adjustments to bridge the gap that now exists between AI and VI. As this new technology slowly engages in our world, more of our activities will be played out in virtual reality. We'll find ourselves spending more time with computers, giving the loads of data to share. We'll communicate through the use of avatars, social platforms, and games.

These virtual worlds will have to be created though, but these are places where it is safe to learn, try, and fail at our attempts to improve. They will take the place of social platforms and make it possible for us to hone our skills in business, finance, and even romance. Whatever you want to test out, there will be a virtual world to work in before you make your idea mainstream.

This will eventually become a fully automated world but not a self-aware world as many people fear. Humans will still set the parameters and put limits on the kind of things they want computers to do. Their intelligent software will be able to simplify and enhance our real life but not take charge and control it. As long as humans put limits on the computer's ability to grow, the future will remain bright for this technological advancement.

Right now, artificial intelligence is still in its infancy, the next decade could be a real eye-opener. Not very far in the future, we will begin to see these machines change the way cars and planes are designed, how they will be operated, and how they will interact with humans. We will watch our days of exploration go further and further into space. In time, we will witness the colonization of new worlds. This time literally.

The future also has many changes in store for a country's military might. Soon, there won't be a need for "boots on the ground" when a country is at war. One soldier will be able to manage an entire fleet of drones that will fight in their place. These are already in use in some partial form now. Called unmanned aerial vehicles or UAVs these drones are capable of being operated from a remote location and responding to a myriad of instructions. In time, these UAVs will become autonomous and work without the aid of human direction.

What does this mean? Imagine a fleet of drones all headed for a single target. If one drone is destroyed by enemy fire, the remaining drones could automatically reassemble and continue on to accomplish their mission. Their ability to learn and grow will allow them to adapt to the function of the destroyed drone and incorporate his assigned task into their programming.

It is expected that with each new system introduced, machine programming will increase in its complexity and capabilities. Today, we think that artificial intelligence is one of the most fascinating forms of technology known to man. What will we think when virtual intelligence becomes available to the mainstream population? These machines will be more capable of interacting with humans and will revolutionize every aspect of our daily life.

Another area where this new technology will improve human life is in the field of disaster response. Areas unsafe for humans to enter can now be accessed by deploying machines to bring aid to people who are cut off from the rest of the world by catastrophic events. Imagine how these intelligent programs can be installed in machines that can search for life underneath the rubble of ruined buildings. How food supplies can be delivered quickly and safely. How rebuilding efforts will be much faster and how the treatment of the injured will be done quickly and efficiently.

We'll see this technology in the movie industry, music, in agriculture, and in an endless parade of other industries as time progresses. Right now, we are pretty sure of what the future holds for a neural network and all of its many applications. What we are not sure of is how quickly humankind will embrace it. No doubt, it will be the younger and more adventurous generation that will embrace it first. They will be the ones to harness its immense potential and they will be the ones who will have to set its limits.

Science has a lot to offer us in the way of advanced computer technology. The machines which will be produced tomorrow and in the years to come will open the door to a whole new world of adventure. But it will happen because people are driven by the powerful force of human desire to always find better ways to do things are stronger than the many who are powerful and in time, they will make the science fiction of the past become the reality of today.

# Conclusion

There is no doubt that we have entered into a whole new era in mankind's industry. Perhaps in the very near future, we will have other artificial intelligence with which we can communicate, to share our ideals and thoughts with. While that time may be far off in the future, it is beginning today. With the aid of neural networks, we now have the power to change the world in many ways.

Neural networks are the very key to the future. No matter what your goals are, what you expect out of life, or what you plan to do, soon, nearly every computer on the planet will be equipped with some sort of neural network. Businesses are using it to improve customer service as well as boost their bottom line. Governments are using it to plan future cities and to better understand the ones we live in today. Other industries are utilizing it to help improve their bottom line, and private citizens also find that even they have a reason to take a closer look at this new and innovative technology. In this book, you've learned a great deal about neural networks.

No matter where you stand, you need to realize that these tiny little machines are going to change your life forever. With the help of this book, you have learned a lot. By now, you should understand what neural networks are and the many algorithms and other components that make it possible for a machine to learn.

You've learned that neural networks are the key component that allows the machine to learn. Without them, the network is simply reduced down to a very basic and simple vending machine that takes in information and then gives you what you want.

But neural networks are far from using such a simple strategy. You also learned the main concepts behind neural networks, the basic architecture, some of the rules and guidelines that have been set to help the machine to learn. You learned about the technical fields and how they operate, and the many different ways that neural networks can be applied in our day-to-day lives.

No doubt, this book has probably raised more questions than answers but it is our hope that we have at least piqued your interest so that you are eager to learn more. There is much to learn on this subject and sad to say, we have barely just scratched the surface.

Regardless of what you expect to achieve with this knowledge, you have taken the first step in your quest to better understand neural networks and their role in our lives today, tomorrow, and well on into the future.

Finally, if you found this book useful in any way, a review on Amazon is always appreciated!

www.ingramcontent.com/pod-product-compliance
Lightning Source LLC
Chambersburg PA
CBHW070855070326
40690CB00009B/1855